WEEKLY READER BOOKS PRESENTS

Matches, Lighters, and Firecrackers Are not Toys

By Dorothy Chlad

Illustrations by Lydia Halverson

WEEKLY READER BOOKS
Middletown, Connecticut

Weekly Reader Books offers several exciting card and activity programs. For information, write to WEEKLY READER BOOKS, P.O. Box 16636, Columbus, Ohio 43216.

This book is a presentation of Weekly Reader Books. Weekly Reader Books offers book clubs for children from preschool through high school.

For further information write to:
WEEKLY READER BOOKS
4343 Equity Drive
Columbus, Ohio 43228

Library of Congress Cataloging in Publication Data

Chlad, Dorothy.
  Matches and firecrackers are not toys.

  (Safety Town)
  Summary: Presents safety rules to be followed when using matches, lighters, sparklers, and firecrackers.
  1. Matches — Safety measures — Juvenile literature. 2. Fireworks — Safety measures — Juvenile literature. [1. Matches — Safety measures. 2. Fireworks — Safety measures. 3. Safety] I. Halverson, Lydia, ill. II. Title. III. Series: Chlad, Dorothy. Safety Town.
  TP310.C53   628.9′22   81-18125
  ISBN O-516-O1982-1   AACR2

Hi ... my name is Jack.

I want to tell you
something. Watch
out for matches ...

lighters ...

firecrackers ...

and sparklers.

They can hurt you.

Matches and lighters have different sizes and shapes. The flame is very dangerous and hot.

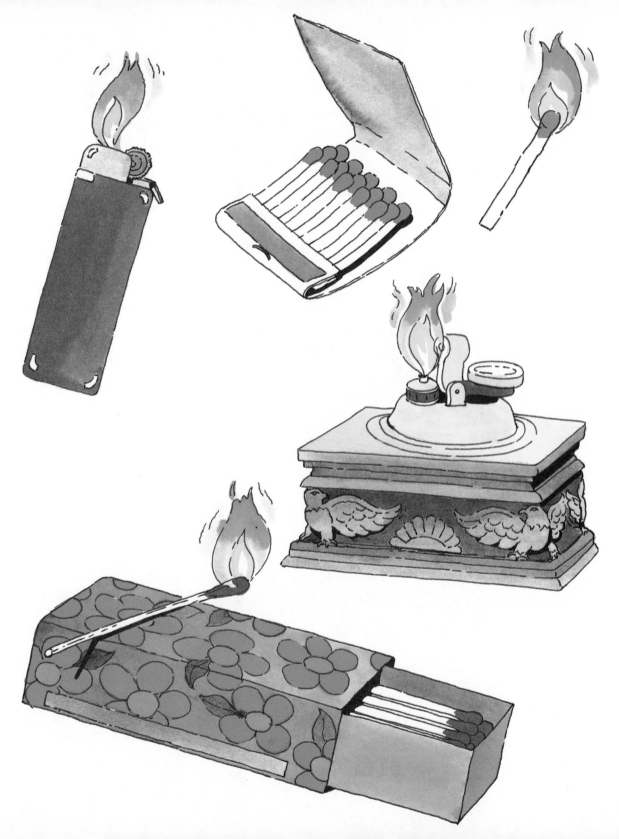

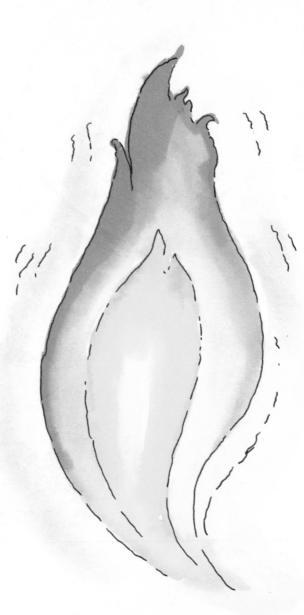

This flame can
start a fire.

Fire can burn you.

Fire hurts many
people and animals.

Fire burns buildings . . .

houses . . .

and trees.

Matches and
lighters are used
for many things.

They can light candles. . .

and grandpa's pipe.

They can light a
fire that keeps us
warm and cooks
our food.

Only big people
can use matches and
lighters. I cannot.

If I find matches,
I give them to
someone older.

Matches and lighters
can start bad fires.

Fires hurt little people and big people.

Some people do not put out their fires.

Their fires can
burn the forest and
hurt many animals.

We make sure our
fire is out before
we leave.

Firecrackers make noise and sparklers are pretty to watch. But they are very dangerous.

Only some people
know how to use
them safely.

Matches, lighters, firecrackers, and sparklers are NOT toys!

My friends and I
never play with
matches . . .

lighters . . .

firecrackers . . . .

or sparklers.

They can hurt us.

Please remember my
safety rules:

Never play with matches, lighters, firecrackers, or sparklers.

When you go
camping, make sure
the fire is out
before you leave.

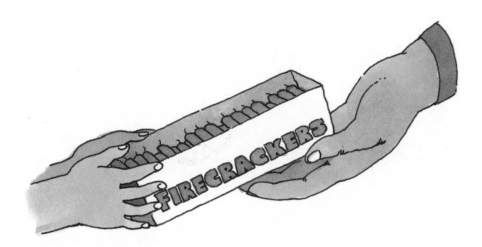

Always give
matches,
lighters,
firecrackers,
or sparklers to
an older person.

About the Author

Dorothy Chlad, founder of the total concept of Safety Town, is recognized internationally as a leader in Preschool/Early Childhood Safety Education. She has authored six books on the program, and has conducted the only workshops dedicated to the concept. Under Mrs. Chlad's direction, the National Safety Town Center was founded to promote the program through community involvement.

She has presented the importance of safety education at local, state, and national safety and education conferences, such as National Community Education Association, National Safety Council, and the American Driver and Traffic Safety Education Association. She serves as a member of several national committees, such as the Highway Traffic Safety Division and the Educational Resources Division of National Safety Council. Chlad was an active participant at the Sixth International Conference on Safety Education.

Dorothy Chlad continues to serve as a consultant for State Departments of Safety and Education. She has also consulted for the TV program "Sesame Street" and recently wrote this series of safety books for Childrens Press.

A participant of White House Conferences on safety, Dorothy Chlad has received numerous honors and awards including National Volunteer Activist and YMCA Career Woman of Achievement.

About the Artist

Lydia Halverson was born Lydia Geretti in midtown Manhattan. When she was two, her parents left New York and moved to Italy. Four years later her family returned to the United States and settled in the Chicago Area. Lydia attended the University of Illinois, graduating with a degree in fine arts. She worked as a graphic designer for many years before finally concentrating on book illustration.

Lydia lives with her husband and two cats in a suburb of Chicago and is active in several environmental organizations.